EXF

C000140714

DISCOVER,

TRANSFORM

HOW TO NAVIGATE CHANGE
AND UNLOCK YOUR POTENTIAL

ALBIE WAKE

Dedicated to anyone with a dream of a better life

FIRST EDITION

TABLE OF CONTENTS

PREFACE

Most of us were afraid of the dark when we were children because that is where the danger is, in the darkness, in the unknown, and what one cannot see. But we are no longer afraid of the darkness of our bedrooms because we have explored them enough to "know-how" to navigate them even in the dark and to know that nothing in our rooms can hurt us when the lights are out.

However, if you were suddenly to appear in the middle of a pitch-black wilderness, the fear would return. And the reason is that its unexplored territory and that's where there are real dangers, real monsters potentially hiding and waiting to kill and eat you. And they would only be a problem because you don't know how to handle them, or how to correctly position and conduct yourself in that environment. The point here is to illustrate the power of "knowhow", and when you don't have anyone to model, and you have a problem that no one has solved before, you must explore. You must explore the unexplored, and the answers will be revealed.

The journey of solving your problems and discovering the know-how to answer the question, "What do you do when you don't know what to do?" will take you into an unexplored territory (into the unknown).

This book will provide insight on how to problem solve and cope with not knowing "how to". Not knowing how to address a situation is an ever-present facet of life, whether it is not knowing what is going to happen, not knowing your worth, not knowing your loved one's values or how to achieve that goal you've always wanted to achieve. There is always an element of the unknown ever-present in life. This book will give you a way of being that will enhance every aspect of your day to day life.

Life is difficult, that is true, but an even greater truth is that we can overcome difficulty.

So who is this book for exactly?

Firstly, if your life is perfect, you're probably able to overcome absolutely every problem you could ever face; therefore, you know enough know-how, then this book is not for you.

If however, you are an ordinary mortal human being, having the usual difficulties, and your current level of know-how is not enough, then you might find this book useful. Remember that the challenges of life threaten all of us at times, not to mention the threat of randomness, unhappiness, corruption, pain and the limitations of the human body. We can be at risk and threatened from all of the above because simply put, we just don't know enough. To blunt: you, as a mere mortal, as a human being, are possibly at constant risk because you're simply too ignorant, too unskilled, and too unaware to not be at risk, and perhaps too dumb to do anything about it! (At least for now.)

So to answer the question "Who is this book for?", it's for those who have problems, or for those who are wanting more, like, "Here I am at space A, and I want to get to space B", and there are difficulties preventing your progress.

So what issues do you have in your life right now?

What challenges do you have?

What difficulties are in front of you?

What problems and obstacles are in your way?

Is it money, or the lack of money? Is it the lack of opportunity, the lack of health, the lack of ability, the lack of support? Is someone stopping you, are you stopping yourself without knowing it? Are you at square one? Maybe it's all of the above, perhaps it's something way more prominent and more significant to all of the above, maybe it's a smaller problem, or maybe you're just bored.

The point is we all have difficulties—big or small—and problems that come in all shapes and sizes. A difficulty is something that needs to be overcome to get you not only what you desire but to live a meaningful life as well. And if you knew how to solve all your problems?

You could be anything you want. You could be healthier, happier, more successful and have more love and meaning in your life. However, your current know-how hasn't quite got you to that paradise life just yet. If you'd like that meaning and that "more" in your life, then this book is for you.

INTRODUCTION

*"No problem can be solved from the same level
of consciousness that created it."*
—Albert Einstein

Life is great, full of love, wealth, health and happiness. It's great if you know how to make it great. If not, life is difficult. It is difficult because you got problems. Having problems is a part of life. Some circumstances barely deserve to be identified as problems, and other issues can be so challenging that identifying them as a problem does not accurately describe the overwhelming difficulty we're experiencing. In life, however, we all experience these things we call "problems", these things that are in between us and what we desire, between us and the great life filled with love, wealth, health and happiness.

A life filled with joy, fulfilment and purpose is essentially a life of consistently solving problems, of overcoming the hurdles and conquering the difficulties. This process of solving problems can be challenging at times, as we don't always have the know-how, and this can cause pain and fear, which in turn can make the experience of life's challenges unpleasant and even overbearing. Not having the know-how itself can become the ultimate problem, as it causes a whole spectrum of negative emotions like fear, anxiety, despair, sadness, not to mention the negative reality that might unfold if we are unable to solve our problems.

On one level of analysis, life is filled with a constant inflow of problems to solve. However, the act of solving problems, depending on the nature and difficulty of the problem, can reward us with a sense of joy, satisfaction, fulfilment, connectedness and success, as well the realization of our desires. All the pleasures of successful living are a result of being successful in life, and being successful is simultaneously being a successful problem-solver.

When we look back, we can often see a series of problems that we either overcame and solved or issues that we did not manage to solve. It might be something we accomplished and looked back on with a sense of pride and joy, or something we might be holding resentment about or feel bitter about because we couldn't find a solution. Or perhaps even when we look around at our day-to-day lives, it can seem like there is a dynamic of problems all around us, at all times, and no matter which way we turn, there seems to be another challenge, another uphill battle, another problem to solve.

Almost all of us to varying degrees attempt to escape our problems, either by avoiding doing something we know we should, by procrastinating or "accidentally forgetting on purpose", or by prioritizing more pleasurable things above finding solutions. We all at some point been guilty of this, avoiding engagement with our problems rather than dealing with them. It may be that our avoidance is all part of our denial and unwillingness to accept that we have a problem or difficulty in the first place.

When we avoid our life's challenges and problems, we create additional suffering and difficulty. Holding ourselves in the problem means we are holding ourselves immersed in fear of that problem as well, and potentially allowing the problem to get worse. All problem solving requires change, and all change brings an element of fear or uncertainty. And nobody enjoys fear.

Because most people avoid problems to a greater or lesser degree, most of us are not living up to our fullest potential. Some of us will even go so far away from our full potential and also seek escapism in the form of video games, T.V., drugs, one-night stands—anywhere we can achieve a total exclusion of our current reality. As I'm sure you know, is not the way to achieve, overcome and be successful with your challenges and problems. What you will discover instead is that avoiding your problems and escaping your challenges will lead you down a road with more difficulty, with more challenges and suffering than the one you are trying to avoid.

Fortunately, we all possess the ability to at least face our challenges and problems. Through encountering these difficulties, we grow and expand ourselves until we are bigger than our challenges, and become able to handle and contend with our challenges, whatever we may face. The knowing how-to part of problem-solving is the essential ingredient required to overcome life challenges and difficulties.

When it comes to solving life's problems and getting to that space that we desire, it comes down to one thing, and that is know-how. "Knowing how" is the essential ingredient to overcoming our challenges and solving the problems we need to address to get what we want and need. Without knowing how or discovering the know-how, we can solve nothing, unless the random chance of luck has reality unfold in a way that happens to be in an exact way, we need and want. With limited know-how we can only get so far with desires, but, with total know-how, we can go all the way without turbulence, overcoming all challenges and solving all problems, perhaps even cheating death.

The commonalities between all difficulties can be conceptualized as a question. This question, if answered correctly, will give the solution to any problem, as it is a starting assumption. The question has been answered by anyone who has ever achieved something beyond their wildest dreams, anyone who has ever overcome something they didn't think was possible or did something they felt they couldn't do.

This question is present in every uncertainty you've ever had, every problem, and it's there with all problems. Whether you don't know how to achieve a particular something or whether you don't know how to attain something. Or maybe you don't know what's going to happen. Or you know what's going to happen, but you don't know how to cope with it.

The point is that you don't know. And that's the problem: *you don't know*. And therein lies the key question:

What do you do when you don't know what to do?

First, let's unpack the question. In a state of not knowing, there is a sense of uncertainty, as you are facing something that is unfamiliar or something that has elements of things that you have not experienced before (the unknown).

Whether it be the unknown of not knowing what will happen or knowing what will happen but not knowing how to cope and deal with it, the critical thing to recognize here is that there is something that is not known. There are blind spots to detect, ways to be found and new things to be discovered.

Now, what do you do when you don't know what to do?

One answer is you do what everyone else is doing. That might be a good solution, because if everyone else is doing it, and everyone else's world isn't falling apart trying to solve their problems and isn't dead, then maybe you should do what they're doing and not die.

The other answer is that you explore the unexplored. Why? Because you might discover a new, more effective how-to that solves your problem. And this is particularly important when what everyone else is doing is wrong, is not working for you or is just not good enough for the situation.

More specific answers to the question, "What do you do when you don't know what to do?" are found in the four sections of this book:

- You use your Values to help you make correct decisions.
- You Explore.
- You embody the Ideal Temperaments.

- You use your already internalized Tools to enhance and accelerate your discovery of the answers and the know-how that you require.

However, the journey of discovery can be a difficult one, as not knowing itself can present new problems. Let's look at concepts that will help.

KEY CONCEPTS

Before we continue, we need a foundation.

Concept A: What, Precisely, is the Unexplored?

> *"There are known knowns; there are things we know. We also know there are known unknowns; that is to say, we know there are some things we do not know. But there are also unknown unknowns – the ones we don't know we don't know."*
> *—Donald Rumsfeld, alluding to the Johari Window*

It's the unknown. It's the unfamiliar. It's uncertainty.

It's new things.

It's what you haven't done before.

It's what you don't know.

It's what you've never encountered or experienced before.

It's reality that exists outside of what your senses can detect.

It's that awful feeling when something catches you unaware.

It's despair and horror when you have been betrayed, because you thought reality was one thing, and it turned out to be something else and that something else was much worse.

It's what you were afraid was under your bed when you were a child (unknown creatures or what a child would call a monster).

It's why some are afraid of the dark.

It's what you don't understand.

It's where you are when you're lost.

It's what you are doing when you don't know what you are doing (confusion).

It's the money problem you can't seem to overcome.

It's the illness you can't seem to recover from.

It's that what you have not thought of.

It's what lies beyond what you know.

It's that which you have not seen, heard, felt, smelled or even tasted.

It's that which you have not experienced.
It's what's inside a surprise.

It's potential.

It's possibility.

It's what you hope for.

The excitement you feel on Christmas morning ("What's inside the box?").

It's that feeling you have when you put on a blindfold.

It's whatever will happen next.

It's an adventure.

It's beyond your wildest dreams.

It's everything you could be and more.

It's that what lies beyond anything you've ever imagined.

Its where the "know-how" is.

The unexplored is always there, just outside our experience. There is always something we don't know, because the universe is big, perhaps infinitely large, and it has an everunfolding field of possibilities, and we are just a small finite part of it. There is a lot to "know", a lot to explore and a lot to discover.

Concept B: Why Do We Fear the Unexplored and Avoid Problems?

"The oldest and strongest emotion of mankind is fear, and the oldest and strongest kind of fear is fear of the unknown."
—H.P. Lovecraft

We fear, resist and avoid the unknown and problems because we are vulnerable; we are vulnerable to things that can hurt us. And the territory where you have not explored, where you don't know what's going to happen is where the danger lies. That's where we don't know where we might not be able to cope and handle, it's where we might fail, lose, get rejected, and as a consequence get hurt in one-way shape or form and even die. So there's good reason to fear, to avoid and to seek comfort within what we know.

However, the universe doesn't just stay on the outskirts of life, sitting statically outside your comfort zone and doing nothing. The world moves whether we move with it or not, and as a consequence, the unknown will inevitably impose itself on us. It will make its presence known.

The world moves whether we move with it or not, and as a consequence, problems can grow and get worse, probably surprising us when we're the least prepared to deal with them. If you hide from your problems, and seek comfort and protect yourself, you will ultimately make yourself more vulnerable to the problem, because you will become older, more ill-prepared, more stuck in your ways and less adaptable. (Or, you can accumulate know-how, even gaining the ability to perceive problems on the horizon.)

So although you might be justified in your fears and have reasons, this is not a valid excuse not to try, not to confront, not to contend, and not to explore the unexplored. You must still move forward into and challenge, because if you don't, as bad and as difficult as your problem is. Life could get worse if you don't try, don't improve, don't make an effort to do something of use or to try to reduce the problems, even if it is just by the smallest of measurable margins.

Whichever way you look at it, despite the fear, we must explore, we must strive to discover and overcome. If you knew (know-how) how to solve any problem you could ever face, you wouldn't fear anything. Then, if you could solve everything, there would be nothing to cause fear, no unknowns to threaten or to hurt and damage you.

So, understanding Concepts A and B, what do we do with this understanding of fear and avoidance?

We increase our ability to discover and acquire how we can handle and can cope with the difficulties and thus dissolve the risk of pain, loss, failure, fear and damage. The only way to overcome these problems in our lives is to go out and conquer them, master them, become so capable that they are no longer considered problems to be fearful of. The key to living a healthy, fulfilling life is to contend and conquer problems.

Our framework will be broken into four parts :

The Problem Solver's Values

The universal values one needs to navigate the unexplored properly.

Exploration

How and why to explore.

Temperaments

The ideal temperaments and outlooks for exploring the unexplored to discover solutions.

Tools

Practices that will improve your effectiveness when trying to discover the way or "know-how" that you require.

I would suggest that you use the material in this book as a companion when you feel the need for some guidance. The content is designed to pick up and select any chapter that stands out to you or that you need throughout your continual growth as a fully functioning person and problem solver.

"A world of possibilities awaits you,
Keep turning the page."
—Oprah Winfrey

THE PROBLEM SOLVER'S VALUES

"All life is problem solving."
—Karl Popper

COMPASS

*"My principles are more important than
the money or my title."*
—Muhammad Ali

Every ship needs a navigator. To aim the ship in the right direction perhaps towards the dry land or away from the stormy seas. As human beings, we are like navigators, navigating our way through life. And all great navigators have a compass, a compass to point them in the right direction.

When you find yourself confronted with a problem, challenged by something or drowning in uncertainty, it is of critical importance to have a personal compass to help you navigate through difficulty and aid in your progress through rough times. But in life, we don't always have a literal compass. Instead, we have values and principles to guide us.

Our lives are directed by all sorts of things, whether it be impulses or basic human needs or our personal goals we can also be guided by our principles, our religious beliefs and our spirituality. Whatever you attribute it to, there is something of value pulling you in one direction or another. This force (your values) that is continuously leading you is behind the decisions you make, and ultimately those decisions have brought you to the place you are now. Therefore, it is your responsibility to yourself to be clear about what is most important in life, value it, and live by it and for it.

In our early years we adopt our caregiver's beliefs and values, but as we grow and develop our sense of self, our values take on a meaning that is unique, based on our own experience of the world. If we want to live a good life with good experiences (the experiences we want and need), we need to live by our values and ideals, constantly and always.

To consistently live in accordance with our values does not guarantee success, but it is our best bet when it comes to operating to our fullest capability in the world. If we don't live by our values, then we betray ourselves by going against what we know to be of more significance (what we hold in higher regard than something else).

And this is how we make decisions, choosing the options that are of more value, that is, of more benefit to ourselves and others. While acknowledging that the details of our circumstance may change, we must be consistent, continually acting in line with our values, or else we will be sabotaging ourselves and weakening our ability to live fully.

It is impossible to live fully if we do not consciously know our values, what we deem important and significant enough to aim at and live by. One of the biggest tragedies in people's lives is that they do not define or own their values, and life becomes pointless and meaningless as a result.

VALUES

"A highly developed values system is like a compass. Itserves as a guide to point you in the right direction when you are lost."
—Idowu Koyenikan

Your values, whatever they are, are the compass that is guiding you. They are shaping your life by guiding you to make certain decisions and take specific actions. Having sharply defined values is exactly like having a moral compass that points you towards what you value most.

Not using that compass intelligently will result in frustration, disappointment, emptiness, and a sense that things could be different. Using it correctly, with the correct and proper values, will result in success, satisfaction, fulfilment, joy and a sense of belonging.

On the one hand an internal sense of discontentment. On the other hand, if you have correct values, when faced with times of uncertainty (for example, when you're surrounded by the unknown), you will experience a sense of certainty, direction, inner peace, and strength of purpose. And having ownership of a moral compass, a value-based guidance system that we can use in times of uncertainty, helps us decide what to do.

The environment or other people will impact us, yet ultimately it is our responses, our own decisions and choices, that cause us our most profound suffering, possibly adding to the pain that might be forced upon us. Of course, people and the environment can hurt us physically, emotionally or spiritually, very deeply, and can affect the course of our lives. But our character, our way of responding and navigating life around the circumstances of the environment or other people becomes the crucia ingredient to having a good life. And our values are what shape those responses.

This superior way of navigating life is with clear values, because this will cultivate self-trust and a good sense of self-confidence that will allow us to explore and to contend with whatever new, difficult or problematic circumstances life might have in store.

This will, In time, help us to develop the know-how to overcome the obstacles in our way. This way of navigating life with strong values will guide us by telling us how we should think and behave, even when things are going wrong, and also when things are going great and according to plan. So as a problem solver, get clear on what is important to you in life, and then do right by it.

UNIVERSAL VALUES

*"You can't build a great building on a weak foundation.
You must have a solid foundation if you are going to
have a strong superstructure."*
—Gordon B. Hinckley

You can start your discovery of the how-to you require by building a solid foundation for the development of a better life, A base of strong, reliable values that you can undoubtedly trust and depend on, no matter what the situation.

No one can tell you what sports team you should like and value, or what colour should be your favourite, or whether or not you should go and buy this instead of that. These are subjective choices and preferences and are unique to you. There are, however, some values that we can all navigate with, no matter what the relative difficulty of our situation or circumstance. No matter our specific circumstances, some values are so universally beneficial that it doesn't seem to matter whether or not you're in the worst place you've ever been or the best place anyone has ever been, these values are still applicable and even needed to some extent or degree at all times.

These universal values will become your internal compass that will help you navigate life. They are the cornerstones of strong ethics, and they do not depend on mood or others behaviour or your environment. They are to be your core values. They are forever, a constant blueprint of how to act. Your foundation values run deep, and they are exact, precise and robust. Your universal values are your foundation that all your success is built on.

People only see the house, not the foundation it's built on. They only see the thriving business, not the effort that created it. They only see the healthy, toned body, not the hours of exercise and good nutrition. These values are the foundation for correct decision making, and when it comes to problem-solving and/ or discovering know-how to solve your problems, sound decisions are crucial. They are what the details of your personal and unique success will be built on. These universal values are basic, simple and foundational for good decisions.

So what are these values? These principles? These navigation points to use no matter the circumstance or the situation?

VALUE #1: DON'T DO THINGS YOU KNOW ARE NEGATIVE

"Nothing in the world is more dangerous than sincere ignorance and conscientious stupidity."
—*Reverend Martin Luther King Jr.*

Here, "negative" means anything that causes unnecessary suffering, pain and hardship. We might not always know what is good or what is the right decision to make, but we are almost always sure of what will make things worse.

Often we can find ourselves faced with a problem, and there are no obvious good decisions to make, or we are in a dilemma. In such cases, it's easy to make matters worse and very difficult to make things better, especially where situations are complicated.

Sometimes all we can do is bear difficulty and endure, and sometimes we have to make unimaginable choices with a terrible price to pay, and the best decision we can make is the one that causes the least amount of suffering.

In these scenarios,

- Don't do what you know will make things worse or decrease or risk the well-being of yourself and others.
- Don't do anything that will not improve things.
- Don't do anything that is unnecessarily risky and dangerous.
- Don't do anything you know will make your life worse tomorrow or in the near term, or anything that will risk or diminish your wellbeing tomorrow or in any future time frame.
- Don't do things that you know you wouldn't do if someone you admired could see you.
- Do not shy away from the truth, and don't lie.
- Don't do anything that is at the expense of someone innocent.
- Don't sacrifice other people for your gain.
- Don't let your inner voice say negative things. Don't say things to yourself that weaken you.
- Don't let bad habits continue.
- Don't indulge in excess. Don't say "yes" when your common sense or your values say you should say "no".
- Don't do anything that you won't forgive yourself for.

As self-evident as it seems to always do what's right for you and to steer away from what is bad, people often don't.

It is very easy to give in to temptation, greed and peer pressure, to give in to excess, indulge too much, etc., at any given time. But don't do it. Your well-being and the safety or security that you're responsible for will always come as a result of you aiming away from what's unnecessarily negative, and your loved ones' and dependents' well-being and safety or security will always come as a result of you aiming away from what's unnecessarily negative for them.

The keyword here is "unnecessary". Avoiding what is unnecessarily negative can be clarified in three distinct sentences:

- Live in a way that does not diminish your well-being.
- Live in a way that does not diminish others well-being.
- Do not live in a way that is good for you now but is going to make your tomorrows worse.

> *"It is wrong and immoral to seek to escape
> the consequences of one's acts."*
> *—Mahatma Gandhi*

VALUE #2: TRUEST TRUTH

"The truth will set you free."
—John 8:32

Truth is reality. The closer we stand to truth, the more accurately we can perceive reality. This value will help you to understand life and reality better, allowing you to accept life on life's terms and putting you in harmony with reality as it is. This accuracy of perception is crucial to problem-solving. You will discover the truest truths by exposing yourself to reality and by seeking to see things as they really are, and not as you want or fear them to be. Dedicating yourself to truth is the fastest way to increase your knowledge and increase your understanding and the know-how that you need.

Dedicate Yourself to the Truth. Seek the Truth. Part of the survival instinct is to avoid what is painful, and so we naturally avoid what is unpleasant. Yet we can make corrections and alterations to our current understanding and know-how only when we have the discipline to overcome that pain involved with exposure to the truth (the reality of the matter at hand). Therefore, we must be totally dedicated to the truth (reality).

This means that we must always regard the truth, as accurately as we can determine it, to be more important, more vital to our wellbeing than our comfort, no matter how painful that truth is. The more we avoid the painful truth, the more likely we are to hold ourselves back (holding ourselves in a naive and incompetent state of being).

To see reality more clearly, you need to continuously make efforts to know the truth and reality for what it is. This sometimes involves experiencing pain because, simply put, the truth can hurt. However, the more truth you can tolerate, the more accurate your understanding will be and the better equipped you will be to deal with life's challenges. Thus you must be bold and even consider your comfort as nonessential when searching for the truth, because the truth is what will reveal the information needed to correct your understanding and relieve your pain.

Speak the Truth. (Be Honest. Be Authentic. Be Congruent. Be Genuine. Be Transparent.) Being dedicated to the truth also means being committed to honesty. It means expressing yourself as honestly and as openly as you can, being clear with your words and your emotions. Be clear with your intentions, be precise with your words, be clear with your behaviour, and when it is time to express yourself, do it as precisely and as honestly as you can.

Trust Yourself. This Includes Trusting Your Judgement of Who is Trustworthy. If you speak the truth and act in a way that is in alignment with the way you speak, and you seek the truth, you will become trustworthy to others. We need to be able to trust others, and others need to be able to trust us in order to survive. To be trustworthy is to be reliable, and the more truthful you become, the more valuable you will become to others. If you seek the truth, the more accurate your judgment will be,and the more you speak your truth, the more trustworthy and valued you will be.

As self-evident as it seems to always speak the truth, act truthfully and seek the truth, people don't. It is very easy to tell white lies, to be vague in your expression and to act in a way that's not in line with how you feel about or understand the world, or even to shy away from truths you don't want to be accept. But don't do that, because your proudest, most respectable, most influential and most transforming moments will always come as a result of you being truthful.

> *"The least initial deviation from the truth is multiplied later a thousandfold."*
> *—Aristotle*

VALUE 3#: MAXIMUM

*"Satisfaction lies in the effort, not in the
attainment. Full effort is victory."*
—Mahatma Gandhi

We cannot (yet) perfectly measure or understand the extent of
our control and influence without trying. We cannot truly know
what is beyond our control and in the hands of fate unless we
define that boundary. We can only find this boundary by giving
100%, all-in effort. Because when we truly give 100% effort, we
can then also define what is beyond our current control.

Then, we must accept what is beyond our control. Not accepting what is beyond our control is the cause of all suffering. Life
might be difficult, hard and painful, but we can always add mis-
ery to the experience by not accepting life on life's terms.

Sometimes the most you can do, and the best thing you can do,
is just to manage. This is like using the headlights on a car on a
dark country road, where all you can see is what is right directly

in front of you. You may not be able to see the whole journey or the road ahead yet, but you don't need to. As long as you know the destination (goal), you can just concern yourself with what you can manage (what your headlights can see and what's right in front of you), and adapt the best you can to the road as it comes.

As you continually give 100%, you will incrementally make things better around you. You will cultivate a sense of progress, and progress is what gives you peace, fulfilment, satiation and enjoyment It's crucial that you make progress and move forward with anything in life, even if you're struggling. Especially when things are tough, when you make progress, you soon cultivate a sense of peace and serenity with yourself and your current position, because you know that you have done all that you can.

As self-evident as it seems to always do your best, people don't. It is very easy to get away with minimal effort and to slack off and be lazy. But don't, because your highest sense of self and the best results achieved will always come from going that extra mile, staying that little bit longer, putting in that little bit more effort and starting that little bit sooner.

So

- Do the best you can.
- Do the most good you can manage.
- Accept what is beyond your 100% effort.

"God grant me the serenity to accept the things I cannot change, the courage to change the things I can, and the wisdom to know the difference."
—Reinhold Niebuhr

VALUE #4: UTILITY

*"Insanity: doing the same thing over and
over again, expecting different results."
—Albert Einstein*

Things have utility because they serve a purpose and are useful. Usefulness is measured by the effectiveness and efficacy something has. Usefulness is what will progress you forward in a better, more effective and efficient way. This is a very "useful" way of perceiving life's challenges, because every challenge has utility, whether things you used to help solve your problems or the experience you can share as a result of an encounter. You must approach life to the best of your ability and make efficiency, that is, focusing on what is useful, one of you guiding principles.

If you're experiencing difficulty now, try to be as effective and efficient as possible. Try to utilize all your available resources to the maximum, whether people, skills, tools or technology (explore your options thoroughly). If solving the current issue is beyond your reach, and it requires more time and effort, try to extract something of value from the experience by realizing something that you didn't know before. A new perspective on the matter is often all that is needed to move forward.

Through exposure to new unseen areas and territory of the problem at hand, you can learn and adapt. Even if your experience does not reveal what you should precisely do next, it will show what not to do and what is *not* useful.

If your problems still haunt you, go over what you did wrong at every decision point. Figure out precisely what you did that was wrong or that could be done better, so you know at least what not to do and, hopefully, what to do instead if you were to reencounter similar events. You must make the changes necessary, so that whatever happened in the past will never happen to you again. Then you will be able to let it go and forget it.

The purpose of abstraction (thinking and memory) is to find utility from them. If you have a persistent memory, see what is of use by exploring the memory from all different perspectives. This will allow you to cultivate a more truthful, accurate and objective view of the reality of the moment. That information will inform you of how to be or how not to be moving forward. The new perspectives of the memory are curative, because you would have extracted the relevant information needed to adjust and learn from it. But you must explore and the memory thoroughly. This is often very painful but necessary to solve the problem, and this is also why "we must value truth more than comfort" (see Value #2).

If you did something to someone else that you feel bad for, you can repent and atone by making amends, by sincerely and thoughtfully apologizing for the things you know you did wrong and/or by fixing what you can. State why you did what you did (not in a justifying way, but in an explanatory way) and **show how** you are not going to make those mistakes again.

If it is a problem that you can foresee happening, then plan and prepare to be as competent and as capable as possible to handle the situation. Schedule, plan, prepare and prepare to adapt, and practice, if possible, to simulate the challenge. Use your time to prepare as much as possible to become the person who this foreseen situation is *not* a problem for.

The more useful and effective you are as a person, the more competent you are. And the more competent you are, the more valuable you become to others and the world. Aim at increasing your capabilities, skills and know-how. Sometimes all you can do to improve yourself or a situation is to just try something, just show up and get involved. Trying is almost always better than doing nothing at all, as, through trial and error, you will discover what is of use and what is not.

To summarize:

- Look for what is useful, effective and efficient.
- Always try to do the best thing, if that is not possible, go to the next best thing.
- Acquire what is useful, effective and efficient.
- Do what is useful, effective and efficient.
- Extract what is of value (what is useful, effective and efficient in serving a purpose).
- Navigate towards useful tools, skills, information, people,

places, and so on that have utility.

- Navigate towards the silver lining of a bad situation (the positive takeaway).
- Navigate towards what you can use to make yourself more effective in moving forward.
- Discard what is useless.

As self-evident as it seems to always do what is effective, practical and most useful, people don't. Instead, they very easily get stuck in their ways, doing what they've always done or what everyone else has always done. But don't make that mistake, because the greatest amount of effect and influence in your life will always come as a result of you aiming for and doing what is most effective and most efficient.

"The most efficient way to live reasonably is every morning to make a plan of one's day and every night to examine the results obtained."
—Alexis Carrel

VALUE #5: DISCIPLINE

"Discipline is being able to force yourself to do something in spite of how you feel, over and over, until it becomes a habit."
—Kim Brenneman

Self-discipline is one of the basic ingredients required to solve life's problems. Without discipline, we can solve nothing. With a little bit of discipline, we can solve a few problems. With total and absolute discipline, we can solve all problems.

Have you ever done something and later on felt guilty and ashamed about? Moments like this are usually due to a lack of discipline, and the antidote is willpower, possessing the willpower to do what you need to do—not want to do, but need to do—without giving in to comfort or pleasure. Valuing discipline and living a disciplined life allows you to progress towards your goals and to actualize them much more rapidly than approaching life with a "one foot on the brakes and one foot on the accelerator" mentality.

A change in thought processes or behaviours, or trying something new, can create anxiety within us, as we cannot always predict the result or feel reassured that what we are doing is correct and beneficial. Yet to willingly confront a problem early, before we are forced by circumstances, will mean that we are able to deal with the issue more effectively, rather than waiting for it to get out of hand. Putting first things first always has a positive outcome. This requires discipline, because staying ahead and on top of problems will not always seem necessary.

- Do what you know you should do.
- Do not indulge with distraction and with comfort.
- When you know enough is enough, stop (know when excess will cause a detrimental effect on well-being).
- Prioritize and concern yourself with what is important and essential.

As easy as it seems to be disciplined, many people aren't and don't exercise such self-control. It is very easy to believe you don't have the willpower and are not capable of such mastery over yourself, but you will see that you do, and you can. Your peace and freedom come as a result of you living a disciplined and self-controlled life that values progress over comfort and laziness.

"Discipline equals freedom."
—Jocko Willink

VALUE #6: RESPONSIBILITY

"The price of greatness is responsibility."
—Winston Churchill

Responsibility is a moral obligation. It's being accountable, taking ownership of your duties or of the things in your care. If you are capable of doing good, and you know that good will come of it, then it is your duty to do so.

Being responsible is also being accountable for your part in what happens to you. It's realizing and accepting that you are part of the cause of what is happening to you, whether you are taking a significant role in causing things to happen or a minor role by just letting things happen and not intervening, not getting involved. There is always a responsibility to be found in any situation. If you are sitting around waiting for somebody to save you, to fix you, to even help you, It will slow your progress and even hold you in a place of self-pity and helplessness.

It must be understood that it is your responsibility to move your life forward, and the sooner it is, the sooner you can change things. It doesn't matter what has happened in the past to you, and it doesn't matter what anyone has done to make things difficult or hold you back. All that matters is how you react to things now, right now at this moment, to take responsibility and move forward with your life. And because we cannot hope to solve and overcome our problems without taking responsibility for them, we must accept responsibility for our difficulties before we can overcome them.

You have infinite potential, therefore you should treat yourself and others if that were true.

- Take care of yourself as you are worthy.
- Take care of your family as they are worthy.
- Take care of your community as it is worthy.
- Take care of your duties like they are worthy of your care.
- Take care of your goals as if they are worthy of achieving.

What exactly does it mean to take care of something? To fix, protect, maintain and nurture something to its best potential self, ability and function. In other words, to take care of your responsibilities. It is very easy not to own or not to hold yourself accountable for something. But don't, because the people we love the most in this world are the people we are responsible for, and the people we most admire are often people that carry the most responsibility. So be responsible.

> *"Being responsible is an enormous privilege....*
> *It's what marks anyone a fully grown human."*
> *–Barack Obama*

VALUE #7: WHY

*"He who has a 'why' to live for can
bear almost any 'how'."*
—Friedrich Nietzsche

Your "why" is your motive. Know why you do what you do. Know your cause, know your justification for your actions. This knowing gives you fuel, and it gives you energy. It provides power to assert yourself. A good enough why will attract social support, and it will give you the capabilities you never knew you had. It will give you a deep understanding. It will give you the energy to discover the know-how you're searching for, and it will give you the patience to persevere, to carry on when others stop.

Your motive for doing something is everything. Your why is going to push you when you can't push yourself when you want to quit and give up your why is going to give you that edge you have, that advantage you need, that lift that you need to carry on and get to the next level. Yes, you might be tired, yes, you might be hungry, yes, your mind might be saying give up, quit; but you will not quit when you will realize that you have not yet reached the goal.

When your self-talk is finding a reason not to, your reason why will say, "This is not what you said you were going to do. This isn't what you talked about. We are not yet there. This is not what you dreamed about. This is not what it looks like." So you'll keep on striving and keep on pushing. You'll keep on fighting, even when feel that you can't, until you win and achieve the dream, the goal, the vision, is all the reason why you must not give up. If you have given up before, it's probably because your reason for going on was no stronger than the reason for giving up.

Ask yourself: Why is it a must for you? Why do you need this? It doesn't have to be extreme, like you've got your back up against a wall, but it has to be strong enough to motivate you, something you're hungry for. One of the only differences in people who succeed is hunger. If you're not hungry and passionate, get around people who are, and their positivity will infect you. Get around people who are doing well and doing better, and you will start to realize that your will power is in direct proportion to the strength of your why.

Universal reasons why:

- To make your life better.
- To improve your loved ones' lives.
- To make the world better.
- To satiate your needs.
- To improve well-being.
- To be who you want to be.

It seems self-evident that we need reasons to be motivated, yet it's easy to just go through the motions and not know why we're doing things. But don't just go through the motions, because your best and most passionate moments will always come as a result of you expressing your passion while trying to address your "why".

> *"A man who hasn't found something he's*
> *willing to die for isn't fit to live."*
> *—Reverend Martin Luther King Jr.*

VALUE #8: FAITH

*"Faith is taking the first step, even when you
don't see the whole staircase."*
—Reverend Martin Luther King Jr.

Faith is not having the know-how but trusting that somehow what you need will happen. Faith is belief in what you can imagine will exist. That's faith, that's all it is, as simple as it sounds, yet more powerful than most people realize and more important to your ability to overcome problems and challenges than words can describe.

Faith is what the future is built on. Almost everything we see once existed only in someone's mind, and eventually it came to be and to exist in the world.

Faith implies that you don't yet know, so you believe that it will be. If you know something, you don't need to believe it, because you know it, you've seen it, touched it, sensed it.

Faith is absolutely essential to not only solving problems, but for your entire life, because without faith, there is no change, there is no progress, and there is no success whatsoever.

Faith is believing in the future, particularly in your aims and goals. Without faith there is no tomorrow. If you see that you're over here in space A (feeling hungry) and imagine space B (food in your belly, full up) and then you make efforts to get yourself fed, there's faith in that. If someone dreamed of a big house, success and achievement, love and joy, there was faith in that too.

Belief literally means to trust, and faith literally means absolute trust. If you trust something absolutely, that means that you expect it to manifest, somehow. Expecting that something will happen is the foundation you can stand on when aiming at something and taking action. If people would only believe in their ability to attain, then and only then one's vision would become inevitable.

The key to having an absolute self-belief is focused imagination and a well-sustained attention. You must continuously and consistently focus on discovering knowhow. By constantly and consistently focusing on mastering that know-how, then the object will happen all by itself. If you are experiencing doubt or fear, or you are letting the negative perception of others bother you, then you are not keeping faith.

You can navigate this world with the truest truths that you currently understand and know, but when it comes to doing things that have not been done before, then you must be loyal to the reality that you can only envision. And if you judge the world by what is possible today, then you delay the possibilities of tomorrow. To create what you can imagine and desire, you must first trust that it's possible and that it will happen.

We have to have faith, because we don't know everything, and so we'll need to take a chance to some degree at some time. We're always jumping into unexplored territory, so having the ability to adapt and overcome is crucial. Having faith in ourselves is the best way to unlock our infinite potential and to overcome and adapt to difficulty and challenges. In this way, believing in ourselves and trusting that we have what it takes to prevail is the foundation of all problem-solving.

You can have **trust** and **faith** in yourself by doing these core things:

- Trust that you are up to the challenge. Before you can discover the know-how, you must first believe it is possible.
- Trust in your ability to adapt,overcome and create what you want.
- Prove to yourself that you can trust yourself.
- Celebrate when your trust is proven correct.
- Find reasons to support your expectations; this will strengthen your expectation, and consequently your trust and consequently your belief.
- Recognize and appreciate the utility you are to others and the world; this will help you recognize some of your capabilities.

It seems so self-evident to just believe in yourself, but people don't. It is very easy to give in to the evidence that it is currently not possible and to succumb to the current understanding of what is possible. But don't your great potential and greatest achievements will always come as a result of you first trusting the fact that it was possible?

> *"If you want to accomplish something, you*
> *must first expect it of yourself."*
> *—Wayne Dyer*

VALUE #9: DO WHAT IS GOOD

*"A good head and good heart are always
a formidable combination."*
—Nelson Mandela

What is good? Good is whatever reduces, alleviates or stop suffering and increases well-being. Always do the best thing you can conceive of doing. Here's a list of things to help you cultivate a strong sense of what is good:

- Take care of your responsibilities and as much responsibility as you can effectively manage.
- Do what is meaningful or what makes a meaningful difference to you or for the good of someone else.
- Do what promotes wellness, or at least what increases your well-being or the wellbeing of another.
- Spend your day being useful and productive.
- Be competent at your job or career; become competent, skilful and sophisticated at what you do and continue to update your knowledge and progress forward.

- Make goals for yourself to achieve Life goals. Yearly goals. Monthly goals. Weekly goals. Daily goals. Personal goals. Family goals. Career goals.
- Do things that improve a better way of life for you and for others, not just now at this moment, but tomorrow and next week and next month, etc. Invest in your future.
- Do the best you can. The best you can do always lies just beyond what you think is your best.
- Do the best thing you can think off. Do the thing that you believe will cause the most good for you and others.
- Be cooperative.
- Act with integrity (consistent, stable, moral behaviour).
- Reciprocate the good that is done unto you.
- Tell the truth. Act so that you can tell the truth about how you act. Live an honest life.
- Pursue what is meaningfully beneficial, not what is immediately gratifying.
- Pay attention. Be mindful of what is going on around and within you. Be mindful of the effect you're having on yourself and others.

- Be considerate. Seek to understand then to be understood. Have empathy and understanding for yourself and
  for others.
- Say things that empower yourself. Encourage yourself
  with your inner voice, and only say things that make you
  feel positive, empowered and strong.
- Maintain and uphold healthy connections
  with people.
- Maintain and uphold your physical and mental health.
- Always consider doing the right thing. And if you cannot
  do the right thing, do the next-best thing.

Ultimately, **Good** can be clarified in four distinct sentences:

- Live in a way that maximizes the well-being of yourself.
- Live in a way that maximizes the well-being of others.
- Live in a way that maximizes the well-being of others
  as well as your own and not at the expense of your own
  wellbeing or at the expense of others (in other words, find
  mutually beneficial outcomes).
- Live in a way that is good for you now and the rest of the

day and tomorrow and next week and next month (effects that grow or at least last for a length of time), etc.

As self-evident as it seems to always navigate towards thegood, people don't. It is very easy to give in to conformityand the easier, more comforting things in life. But don't, because your greatest rewards and most significant effect on the world will always come as a result of you aiming forwhat is good and making the right choices.

"Do what's good for you, in a way that's also good for your family and if you can manage it, in a way that's also good for your community, in a way that is good for you now and tomorrow and next week and next month and next year."
—Jordan Peterson

NAVIGATE

*"Your brains in your head. You have feet in your shoes.
You can steer yourself in any direction you choose."*
—Dr Seuss

Know that you know the universal values, with which you can navigate well no matter what situation. Consider these values and navigate life with them in mind. No matter what difficulty, no matter what problem life has thrown your way that might seem threatening, you can embody these values through your behaviour. You can always be a beacon of truth. You can always do the most good that you can. You can always extract something of use from an experience. You can always be disciplined and do something you know you should, even when you feel you don't want to. You can always navigate well.

- Don't do **negative** things.
- Do the **most** you can, always.
- Do what is **useful** and effective.
- Speak the **truth**, act the **truth** and seek **truth**.

- Take as much **responsibility** as you can manage.
- Have **discipline** and put in the effort.
- Understand **why** you're doing things.
- Have **faith** in yourself.
- Do **good** things always.

The problem-solving power that comes from these principles is a foundation and will help you unlock your potential. By centring your life on these timeless, unchanging values, you can create a foundation for living a good, rewarding and fulfilling life. All other skills, methods, ways and techniques are built upon these central values.

By having those values at the heart of all you do, you can move in the world in a way that is correct, that facilitates development and that allows you to transcend your problems by becoming someone who can handle them. Living with these values is a great self-nourishing, selfcorrecting way of overcoming difficulty. Then, no matter what form your challenge may take, you will remain centred with your universal values.

PROBLEM-SOLVING

*"You can tell the size of a man by the size of
the thing that makes him mad."*
—Adlai Stevenson

Know-how is the basic ingredient we require to solve life's problems. Without knowing how we cannot solve anything. However, we now at least know what direction to move using our internal compass of universal values.

No matter what life throws your way, whether it be the tiniest of problems (for instance, "What should I eat tonight?") or at the other end of the spectrum, being struck by a combination of awful catastrophes.

A person without values is a lost, aimless soul, and the weaker the values, the weaker the individual's mental state. Ultimate values equals ultimate internal strength, because no matter how lost you feel, how helpless it may seem, you will always be able to orient yourself in the right direction with correct values.

EXPLORATION

"We shall not cease from exploration and at the end of exploring will be to arrive where we started and to know the place for the first time."
—T.S. Eliot

EXPLORE

*"Just try new things. Don't be afraid. Step out of
your comfort zones and soar, all right?"
—Michelle Obama*

What do you do when you find yourself in the dark? You turn on the lights. What do you do when you don't know what to do? You **explore**, so that you can discover what not to do and what to do.

When you're faced with an overwhelming problem, that you don't know-how to solve, what do you do? The answer, again, is that you **explore**.

Yes, maybe you could do what everyone else is doing, but not if what they're doing is not actually good enough for you or is not actually solving the problem, or if perhaps it's a problem that no one has solved before. Again, the answer is: you **explore**. You **explore** your options, you **explore** unexplored territory, you **explore** the unknown, you **explore** yourself, you **explore** others, you **explore**, **explore**, **explore**! And stay open to other possibilities, because you might need to **explore** them too.

This is how you discover the know-how that you need in order to solve and overcome whatever it is that is bothering you. Your exploration is just like turning the lights on in the dark. The light shines directly into the darkness and makes the unseen, seen, and exploration into the unexplored is making the unknown, known. You **explore** so that you can become aware of what you are not aware of, just like turning the lights on in the dark allows you to see what you could not see.

The reason for exploration is simple. So you can have practical contact with the part of reality that you are yet to experience and understand. And in your exploration, you will observe facts and events within that new territory and begin to cultivate knowledge and skills (know-how) in order to utilize and solve your problem. This will allow you to have a more beneficial and optimal experience of life, with the least amount of unnecessary suffering possible and the most amount of pleasure, joy, happiness and fulfilment. You explore so you discover and grow, so you don't have to suffer from what has entered your experience and disturbed you. You explore so you don't have to suffer more than you already are dealing with managing your current difficulties.

And if you're exploring new territories (space you've yet to e xperience), then you're very likely to discover the answers and the resources you need, even sooner than you might think, depending on how much you uncover. (A little side note: the answers you need to solve your problems are not always the solutions you *want*, but the solutions you *need*.) Once you encounter the reality of a situation by exploring it and seeing clearly it for what it really is, you will be informed by the experience, and the new perspectives gained will become a part of you. Additional realizations will be made, and you will begin to cultivate the knowhow and begin to transcend the unique problems at hand.

By continuously exploring your difficulties, you will be informed of all the ways something does and doesn't work. From there, by testing solutions, you can adjust, formulate and strategize in real-time, becoming someone who is capable of handling the problem to the extent that it is not a problem at all.

If life isn't what you want it to be, then you can let go of ineffective ways of doing and thinking about things, trading that for the person you could become by exploring new ways of doing and thinking about things. New ways and new territory will help this transformation. All you have to do is:

- Experience new space (unexplored territory),
- Be willing to experience the areas of unknown, and
- Bear the uncertainty when you don't have the know-how to solve your problem.

These phases are necessary to find the know-how, so that you can solve those new problems.

POSSIBILITIES

"Until you cross the bridge of your insecurities, you
can't explore your possibilities."
—Tim Fargo

You do not have to go out into the world and expose yourself to things you haven't done before in order to explore. You can go on an explorative adventure without actually going anywhere, because you're a creature capable of abstraction. That's what thinking is: exploration within the world of thought. That's what thinking evolved for, so that you can explore new ideas and ways of going about things in your mind, so that you don't have to suffer the consequences in real life in order to discover what is useful or learn the "hard way".

Good thinking is exploration of things you haven't specifically thought of before—that is, thinking of solutions—in order to discover something better and more useful. That's also what a good conversation is: two or more people thinking together about things, talking (exploring) about a topic, sharing perspectives and, at the same time, gaining each other's perspectives. And at the end of the conversation, each comes away a little better off than before.

And in doing so, in exploring things out in the world or in your own mind or a good conversation, you will gain new perspectives. And if you gain new perspectives, you're likely to get new understandings. And if you acquire new understandings and understand something a little better, you're more likely to discover the know-how you to solve your problems. The fundamental premise of psychotherapy, too, is that if you talk freely (explore) about what's bothering you (problems), you will gain a new perspective and new understandings; these understandings will then lead to new solutions and ways to equip yourself better to cope with your situations. And that's the primary goal of psychotherapy: better coping.

The primary way of coping, that is, of becoming a good problem solver, is through exploration and shifts in perspectives. Problems are simply evidence that something could be improved. A good place to start exploring improvements is precisely *in the direction of what you are finding difficult* (see the section on "Tools" for more knowhow). That's where there will be something to be discovered, something to be understood, something you have not encountered or some way of perceiving things that you are yet to perceive.

Or maybe that's you have already encountered and discovered the crux of the problem, but have not yet dealt with it in a competent and effective way. Perhaps some of the subtleties and nuanced ways need to be discovered. In this case, too, problems stem from "the unknown" (not knowing how to cope or solve), and, as we've already established, the unknown solution can be found exploring yourself, the environment and talking with other people.

To overcome your difficulties, you need to confront the unknown willingly (the unexplored areas), which laces and surrounds your understanding. Immerse yourself in those unexplored spaces and explore all possibilities and options that you can, so that you can discover and absorb whateve information nourishes your understanding of the matter at hand and develops the know-how you need. Pay close attention to the information you attain, and you will transcend the problem with your adjustments and improvements. Start with looking at your errors (for example, approaches, assumptions, behaviours, strategies), and sacrifice them in order to become better than what you are. Then you can start changing the things around you as well. In this way, voluntarily exposing yourself to the unknown (unexplored problematic areas) is curative, in the sense that the cumulative experience facilitates the growth of your understanding and generates solutions that benefit yourself and others.

See your exploration as adventure, because that's what it is. It's a transformation process, it's a creative process, and it's converting the unknown into the known and simultaneously dropping away old useless parts of yourself and adding new more improved ways. It's going from uncertainty to certainty via the path of experience and understanding. From the unexplored to the explored, mapped and understood. From not knowing to knowing.

And this is achieved by doing things differently than before. This doesn't always mean drastically and radical jump straight in at the deep end of the pool kind of exploration. It can mean subtle and nuanced differences that get explore. Exploration, at any level, is still exploration.

IMPROVEMENT PROCESS

"There is nothing noble in being superior to your fellow man; true nobility is being superior to your former self."
—Ernest Hemingway

You are what you can transform.

You may not be capable of success with certain things right now, but human beings are certainly capable of transforming and growing. And you are most definitely capable of transforming into someone capable of succeeding, if only you explore the unexplored and learn. In doing so (exploring) you will become informed by what you are exposed to. As a result, you will be able to change and alter yourself and your environment in a way that better suits your new more well-informed self and your values, and better represents your intentions with more sophisticated applications.

In order to improve, do not shy away from problems; instead, accept them, confront them, become bigger than they are by learning from what you encounter. By exposing yourself to new ways of doing things is both experiencing more of reality and, therefore, cultivating a deeper and broader understanding of what is true.

When progressing towards your vision for life, you will likely experience setbacks and learning curves, but you must stumble forward towards your goal, through the unfamiliar (unexplored). As you are doing so, you will attain new information, becoming familiar and discover what to do or what not to do, and you will find that small micro goals will pop up (smaller problems to solve). In this way, you will solve them and move towards your big goals in a zigzag fashion, edging closer and closer to a solution. Constantly adjusting, calibrating, refining and improving (by discarding and dropping old ways and parts of yourself which are useless and adding or acquiring what is useful, you will develop yourself with a high degree of complexity and effectiveness.

Remember: no one's knowledge can go too far beyond their experience, so exposure to the unexplored territory is essential to improvement!

Here is a little overview of how people get better and improve via exposure to new things, steps that anyone can use to get better at something, especially when it's exploring new territory:

Prepare, engage, analyse, calibrate, reengage.

That's it, and it's that simple if you want to improve yourself more than you already are.

Procedure Preparation

This is where you prepare yourself as well as you possibly can to face the upcoming challenges. Then you...

Engagement

This is the stage where you engage the task at hand full-on, get involved, immerse yourself and get stuck in and explore (see "Temperament" for more detail). Actively try to achieve the goal (discover solutions to the problem). Being proactive, and open to the experience is critical in this stage of the process of attaining your vision, because unless someone miraculously goes out and achieves your goals for you or discovers the solutions for you, then you're not going to achieve or discover.

Analysis

This is where you examine key events, key moments by going over what you did wrong and right at every little decision point, identifying errors and critical areas that you can improve. Figure out exactly what you could do better, so you know at least what not to do. This is how we improve, by figuring out what does work and what doesn't work and letting go of what doesn't. Then, eventually, we are left with what does work, and we can repeat it and improve it and add new ways and approaches into the mix. Also, identify the lost potential of that moment, and then let it go by extracting relevant and useful information and recognize the new possibility of the next moment. Don't get stuck in the past potential, wishing to relive that moment. Move forward into the new potential of the next moment and look forward to the great adventure.

Calibration

On the other side of event analysis, having analyzed and made the necessary improvements, you adjust, improve, adapt and re-orient yourself and prepare yourself to reengage. After reviewing the situation or event you've just encountered, and assessing what you've learned, now you have new information, and you are more able to adapt, calibrate and make the necessary adjustments, so the errors of the previous event are less likely to happen again. Then you can move forward with more sophistication and knowhow than before.

Re-engagement

Engage again, only now from a more well-informed perspective. To be informed means to be in the proper position in relation to what the environment has previously shown you works and doesn't work with regards to the goal. You can also calibrate and navigate more effectively on the fly in the moment-to-moment action, learning and adjusting in real-time.

Electricity is incredibly dangerous, and if you interact with it incorrectly, it can even kill you. But if you know what you're doing and interact with it correctly (if you are sophisticated and well-informed), it can power the world. Again, the difference is the know-how. This is what being informed means: knowing "how-to" compared to not knowing "how-to".

As you experience more and more of what you don't know, incrementally, your judgement will encompass a broad spectrum of consequences and will reflect a wise balance and quiet assurance. The more you re-engage, the less often you will have to struggle, change and calibrate at every mistake point, because you will be improving yourself.

Because you will be more sophisticated you will be making less hefty mistakes. This improvement process is fundamental because we are finite creatures who are riddled with needs and desires that must be addressed. We have to learn and improve, cultivate and acquire in order to survive.

So now that we understand this, one way we can look at our challenges, difficulties and problems is, in a sense, like a learning process. At the end of that process, we will be better and more well-informed than before. Our setbacks and so-called failures will help us navigate our way to the solutions, methods and successful approaches needed to get us into space where our problems and challenges are no longer overwhelming.

"Any opportunity given, should be taken seriously."
—Kevin Hart

SOPHISTICATION

"It's only after you've stepped outside your comfort zone that you begin to change, grow, and transform."
—Roy T. Bennett

Sometimes when your way of doing things works well, you might be tempted to always behave that way, especially when everything is going as you expect. However, sometimes your old way of behaving won't work. No matter how familiar something seems, differences, as subtle they might be, appear in a seemingly repetitive routine. Even if this isn't the case, every moment is itself unique.

If your particular way is not working or is not going to plan, then your method is not completely accurate, and your ways of doing things can be improved. This is why no matter what we know, no matter what experience we have attained and what ways we have learned, we must always bring a sense of mindfulness to the event (see more in "Temperaments"). We must always be open and interact in a way that facilitates growth and allows for a deeper and broader sense of understanding.

The world isn't in a static state, and it is continually changing and growing, and so are people. So we must grow and change and constantly update our ways of being, so that we are always on the proper path, operating optimally and fully in harmony and up to date with the ways of the world.

The more sophisticated and experienced you become the more specific and precise your aim will develop. You will develop to a high degree of complexity in all your ways of interacting, under-standing and behaving, so that you are continuously progress-ing in life, observing larger patterns of cause and effect in your problem-solving. This is "crystalized intelligence", and it allows experts and older adults to entirely avoid problems by tapping into a lifetime of accumulated experience and life hacks.

As you become more and more sophisticated over time, you will be able to home in and navigate life's problems with ever more rapid adjustment and calibration, steering yourself properly and accurately through your problems. There will be more internalized know-how that you can map onto the new and unexplored experiences. This background knowledge can allow you to more reliably focus more on the subtle, finer and nuanced details of your discoveries.

It's a little like when you first learn how to drive, consciously thinking about every little thing. Turn here, look here, mirror, indicate, brake then select gear, look both ways then go, etc. However once driving has been experienced a few times, those ways of behaving become internalized, and all of the above becomes second nature. You don't have to think about any of that at all. Before long you're no longer concentrating on basics, and you can focus on other, finer details of driving, like what is being said on that podcast you're listening to or how much fuel is left.

As you explore, you will cultivate a high degree of complex understanding, as well as judgement that encompasses a broad spectrum of long-term effects and consequences of your decisions. In this way, you will acquire a better sense of what the right decision is. You will begin to see things differently, and thus you will think and act differently too.

Your effect on your world is limited only by your understanding and observance of natural laws, ways of the world and the correct principles, methods and approaches for interacting with whatever it is you're interacting with properly. After exploring and overcoming your current problems, you will interpret all of life's experiences to some degree in terms of opportunities for learning and contribution, whether it be for your benefit or the benefit of others.

SPACE-A, SPACE-B

"Without dreams and goals, there is no living, merely existing, and that is not why we are here."
—Mark Twain

When exploring and "sophisticating" yourself, it's critically important to have an outcome in mind, a goal, an aim, a vision, some ideal future you want or need to be experiencing. Call it what you will, you must have goals, desires and a vision of what you want, and drive towards these aims. Otherwise, your path will lead to stagnation, decay, meaningless and purposeless existence. It's the process of achieving or attaining our goals that gives life its meaning and purpose, and a drive to overcome and solve the problems and obstacles between you and the desired outcome.

Most people aim badly (but aiming badly is so much better than not aiming at all!). The best is to aim well. Define your outcome that you want and move forward towards your goals as you explore.

Envision this: here you are, at Space-A, and you have a vision of where you want to be at Space-B. Space-A is where you are, your current environments and problems, and who you are, what habits and daily routines you have, what methods and ways you use to cope and handle your difficulties and problems. Space-B is where you want to go, or what you want to happen. Space-B is what you want to be, it's what you value. It's where all your needs get met, it's the goal and the vision. Space-A is reality, as it actually is right now. Space-B is the place you regard as better than where you are now, where you find all problems solved, and goals achieved. It's the future. It's possibility. It's the potential that you want.

A good way to know where exactly you are (Space-A) is to simply pay attention. People often do not recognize where they are, because, simply put, they are not acknowledging the situation they are in. Specifically, the don't realize their contributions to staying stuck, the path they are on and where it will lead until it's too late. To not realize your potential and the opportunities that surround you until it's too late is a great tragedy, so pay attention.

To pay attention, just seeing yourself and your surroundings what they objectively are, simply tune in to all your senses. Using your instincts for truth and your understanding (see the section on "Universal Values") distinguish your surroundings, where you are and precisely the direction you are going. Then you will have a grip on Space-A and a much better sense of Space-B (where you want to go). Even a satellite navigation system doesn't work unless it knows where it is and where it's going.

Again, Space-B is the vision and goals, and between where we are now and that goal, problems arise (in other words, we don't know how to achieve or find solutions as desired). This is the space we need to explore and navigate through, towards where we want to be. This is why it's so important to get a clear vision of Space-B. If the vision is clear, and the goal is worthy enough, then no matter how many obstacles are in your way or how difficult they are, you always have a sense of direction and a reason to move forward and bear the challenges and burdens ahead. Vision is the highest quality of the explorer. Vision is the ability to see Space-B and see all obstacles in your way clearly. No matter what problems you are faced with, you must always move in the direction that will edge you closer and closer to the goal. To identify your shortcomings (the unknowns), to explore and attain the know-how in order to conquer your problem and actualize the vision gets you to Space-B.

In addition to Space-A and Space-B, there is also Space-C, and that's the future time frame where you don't want to go. Space-C is usually a degraded, aged and battered, weaker with less potential and more difficult version of where you are (Space-A). This is where you will inevitably end up if you do not progress towards a better space, the goal (Space- B).

> *"Between stimulus and response*
> *is the freedom to choose."*
> —*Victor Frankl*

Often people end up in Space-C because they didn't realize exactly where they were in relation to where they wanted to be. Perhaps they continually procrastinated and/or tried to escape their problems. Perhaps they avoided the dreaded exposure and exploration of the problems and difficulties, and the struggles involved in solving them and overcoming the obstacle. Perhaps at some level they decided that their current routine was more comfortable, expediently rewarding and pleasurable than the journey and exploration involved in reaching the better space, the vision of Space-B.

A good place to start with on this journey towards the goal is to begin by identifying what you're doing that's keeping you where you are, what contributing to this problem and what do you need to 'know-how' to do in order to solve this problem, what's the unknown (the unexplored area) here that needs to be explored in order to hone in on the 'how too'. Where are you trying to go, what's changing around you, what do you need to engage with and expose yourself too in order to learn.

Conceptualize yourself as a process, not as a static state. Because as soon as you reach Space-B, at the same time the goal materialized, it becomes the new Space-A (our present reality as it is), and then new problems will arise. We then must re-orient ourselves and navigate towards a new vision (a new Space-B), or we will end up in an experience that we don't want (a stale, monotonous, Space-C).

You must continually calibrate and reorient yourself as best you can towards a new goal, or you will inevitably end up experiencing a goalless, purposeless and meaningless existence. And, as we've said, the antidote to this is having an aim, a goal, something to strive for. Because we don't want to end up in a meaningless, problem-avoiding, pointless state of experience (Space-C). So we must always be open and interacting in a way that facilitates growth and allows for a deeper and broader sense of understanding, so we can solve our problems and progress towards our goals.

The world isn't in a static state, but continuously changing and growing, and so are people. Therefore we must grow and change and constantly update our understandings and ways of being and behaving, so that we are always on the proper path, becoming what we can be, fulfilling our potential and operating optimally, growing optimally with goals and aims (see section on "Universal Values"). No matter what we know, no matter what goals we achieve, status we reach, experience we have or ways we have learned, we must always bring a sense of mindfulness to each event, a sense of openness. No matter how much we think we know, there is always something to be explored, something that could be done better, or something to be solved.

CONCERN

"Focus. Otherwise, you will find life will become a blur."
—*Unknown*

With a clearly defined vision (or aim or goal) focuses our efforts on things that are related to the vision. We need to be concerned about and to work on things that bring us closer to the realization of that goal. The nature of our energy is then focused and concerned only with what is relative to the aim.

In contrast, without a clearly defined vision and outcome in mind, we focus our efforts on whatever irrelevancy presents itself from moment to moment. We focus on the weak, un-empowering things that have no positive contribution to our progression towards the goal. As long as we are working with the "universal values" in our hearts and aiming at our goals and visions, we can empower our lives.

You can only experience the joy of achievement and success by having a focus and achieving that goal or progressing towards that aim. Then your body will release all the feelgood emotion needed to reinforce you on that path towards your vision, while solving the problems between Space-A and Space-B, but you must have a clearly defined aim or aims. It is only when you focus on what is relevant to the goal that you can prioritize and structure your efforts, and know what to focus on and what to spend your energy on.

> *"You will never reach your destination if you stop and throw stones at every dog that barks."*
> *—Winston Churchill*

Your ambitions and goals can act much like a flashlight illuminating specific portions of reality. By making a goal (Space-B), you will begin to look at the world in terms of things that hinder your progress towards your goals, versus ideas that are of use and help you progress towards your goals. *And everything will be relatively important to the degree that they are of use or are an obstacle to the achievement of the goal.*

Because of this focus, your ambitions and goals will also simultaneously make you blind to everything else, making most things irrelevant. So be very careful what you wish for, and make sure it's worth sacrificing your sensitivity to everything else. It is crucially important to choose your goals wisely, because you could already be exposed to wonderful opportunities that are right in front of your face that you don't recognize because of your focus on incorrect goals.

> *"The successful warrior is the average man,*
> *with laser-like focus."*
> *—Bruce Lee*

TEMPERAMENTS

*"Attitude is a little thing that makes
a big difference."*
—*Winston S. Churchill*

THE IDEAL TEMPERAMENTS

"When you take control of your attitude,
you take control of your life."
—Roy T. Bennett, The Light in the Heart

The ideal temperament of a great explorer of the unexplored are the moods and attitudes that best promote the discovery of solutions and facilitate self-growth as well as the overcoming and solving of problems. These temperaments are the optimal characteristics and attitudes that anyone can embody when exploring the unexplored. These temperaments will become your go-to attitudes when faced with difficulty, whether your problem has come entirely out of the unknown or you are pro-actively exploring new territory.

So what are these temperaments? These attitudes? These characteristics we can embody when faced with difficulty, and we need to explore in order to find the way? Let's find out.

TEMPERAMENT #1: OPENNESS TO EXPERIENCE

"The mind is like a parachute: it doesn't work unless it's open."
—Unknown

Openness to experience is being receptive to new information, new ways, new possibilities and new experiences. Openness, in turn, cultivates a broader perception of the world, leading to a deeper understanding and more informed choices and objective decision-making, allowing evaluation through a wider lens of perception. Openness is an attitude present in all of the highest achievers in the history of humankind, to boldly go into the unknown and unexplored. This willingness to experience life, in the moment-to-moment unfolding, whether it be a success or a failure, an essential characteristic for exploring new things.

To be receptive to the unknown, to be receptive to the discovery of the know-how you require, you have to be open to the challenges of life and be willing to experience difficulty and setback and failure from time to time. In addition, to be effective at problem-solving, it is necessary that your ways of problem-solving be truly open for inspection by the world, and that they be tested, whether this comes in the form of criticism from others, embarrassment and failure, etc. You must be totally dedicated to the fact of reality, and that means living honestly and openly. Increasing your openness to experience is vitally important to solving life's problems.

Openness to experience is playful, and it is experimental. It is experiencing the full spectrum of emotions as you willingly explore. Openness to experience is the opposite of close-mindedness and defensiveness. It is being completely willing to fully experience whatever we are actively exploring.

If someone is close-minded and defensive, it usually means that they are responding to the experiences as if it is threatening in some way. They attempt to temporarily render threatening experiences harmless by distorting their awareness or denying the experience. A large part of the process of exploration, though, is the continuing discovery of what you are experiencing (feelings and attitudes) which, before now, you might not have been aware of.

To embody openness, you will need to replace defensiveness and rigid ways doing things with increasing openness to experience and to new ways. You will then become more openly aware of your own feelings and attitudes, because you will express and explore them more often, as well as being aware of opportunities than you would otherwise. You will become more aware of reality, as it exists objectively, outside of yourself. This is because you will be more likely to have gained a vast number of different perspectives, because you have experienced new territories, new people and new ways more often.

Your awareness will include the details of life, in greater resolution, as well as the bigger picture. You will notice that not all days are the same, that not all problems are "problems" but opportunities, and that not all bad people are "bad" but are unaware. You will be more able to take in the information in a new situation, as it is, as opposed to distorting it to fit a preconceived category or set ways of looking at the world.

Increasing your ability to be open to experience will make you far more realistic in dealing with new people and new situations. Because your beliefs are flexible, you will tolerate ambiguity, and you will receive conflicting evidence without forcing closure.

This openness of awareness to what exists at this moment, within yourself and in unexplored territory, is an extremely important element not only for the person who discovers solutions, but for the most successful people who ever lived. Being open-minded is, at the same time, having humility, which means that you are open to learning. It allows you to receive new truths and new information that you would otherwise reject.

To summarize:

- Stay open to the possibilities.
- Be willing to experience all the visiting emotions that come with the new experience.
- Be willing to experience what the new space has to offer.
- Be willing to be challenged and tested, and, if necessary,

be willing to fail and be wrong.

- Be humble and be willing to accept that others might know something you don't.

"The only source of knowledge is experience."
—Albert Einstein

TEMPERAMENT #2: COURAGE

"Success is not final; failure is not fatal; it is the courage to continue that counts."
—Winston Churchill

Courage is the willingness to experience fear, uncertainty, pain and danger and to do what is right to achieve the greater outcome. When exploring new territory, your emotions can stifle you, particularly fear, which is why it's necessary to have courage. Courage means going into the new territory and experiencing the unknown and the unexplored despite all the anxiety you might be experiencing.

Courage does not mean fearlessness; it means pressing on despite the fear. Living courageously will eventually lead to fear being replaced with absolute trust in yourself, knowing that you will be okay. If you continuously live courageously, slowly you will replace fear and uncertainty with certainty and self-assuredness and belief in yourself.

When you go into new territory, into the unexplored, and it can be immense. This is because you don't know what is going to happen, or you do know what will happen, but you don't know how to handle it. If you are experiencing fear, you are probably leaving your comfort zone, the zone of predictability, and are now doing things you've not done before or experiencing things you've not experienced before. Sometimes the fear can be justified based on the level of danger and risk and further harm that you are facing, but that is not what courage is about. It's is about moving forward and doing the best you can despite the fear, and striving for the goal, no matter what negative emotions you're feeling or what risk of physical harm might be involved. You will use your judgement (see section on "Universal Values") to chart the best possible course.

To accept the challenge of the new, unexplored territory and to contend despite all fears and risk, is courage. In one sense courage is risking the known for the unknown, it's risking the familiar for the unfamiliar, the comfortable for the uncomfortable. Courage pulls you into the unknown and unexplored and forces you to learn and adapt.

"One moment of courage can change your day. One day can change your life. And one life can change the world."
—*Mel Robbins*

TEMPERAMENT #3: CURIOSITY

*"There's never a chance that we'll run
out of things to explore."*
—Sylvia Earle

Curiosity, or the desire to know or to learn, has been attributed over thousands of years as the driving force behind not only human development, but the developments in science, language, and the industrial world. They say curiosity killed the cat, but it also discovered the lightbulb. When you are experiencing a gap in your knowledge, curiosity kicks in, and you then begin to feel motivated to fill in the gap of understanding.

Curiosity is a sort of appetite. Much like feeling hungry, which can only be satiated when you eat, curiosity is only satiated with the know-how that you require. This is much like your relationship with food, in which you can only satiate your hunger when you eat, and that satiated feeling only lasts so long, until you need to eat again. A good method for sophisticating yourself in any new territory is to become insanely curious (that is, insanely hungry). You will get curious when there is a gap in your understanding, particularly when you need know-how or to understand how something works. When you discover the know-how, you will be satiated, until another gap in your knowledge inevitably comes to your attention.

Curiosity is a powerful and positive emotion that can fuel your quest for discovery. Discovering new information is inherently rewarding and pleasurable, because it can help reduce undesirable states of uncertainty and anxiety. And the reduction of these unpleasant feelings, in turn, is rewarding, not just because of the pleasant experience of stress reduction, but because you are more likely to operate fully, and, therefore, more likely to explore and discover.

When you are disrupted by something unfamiliar, uncertain, or ambiguous, it is the characteristic of curiosity that drives you to gather information and knowledge of the unfamiliar and to restore coherent thought processes, so that you are better able to solve your problems. Embodying curiosity will create a desire in you to make sense of unfamiliar aspects of your environment and problems through interaction (that is, exploration).

By exhibiting curious and exploratory behaviour, you can gain knowledge of the unfamiliar, and, as a result, reduce the state of uncertainty or unpleasantness. Replacing your fear of the unknown with curiosity, and specifically aiming that curiosity at what is causing that fear, can only be good for you; curiosity will help you home in on that which is of value in the new territory (so that you can cope). Curiosity keeps leading into the new, so let yourself investigate, because knowledge of reality enables mastery of reality. Of, if not, at least you will be someone who is actively trying to get better.

As we know, it is not a good idea to ignore or shy away from problems and difficulty. Do not wait to investigate and prepare for upcoming problems; instead get curious and explore your potential solutions. Not only will you be more likely to solve your problems, but perhaps can prevent them before they even arise.

Curiosity is inherently rewarding, constantly flooding you with positive emotion, rewarding you more with and more with every bit of useful new information you acquire. So stay curious. It's what keeps us alive. Curiosity will, if embodied and practised, become your most rewarding state of being

"Curiosity, especially intellectual inquisitiveness, is what separates the truly alive from those who are merely going through the motions."
—Tom Robbins

TEMPERAMENT #4: PATIENCE

"Continuous effort – not strength or intelligence – is the key to unlocking our potential."
—Winston Churchill

While exploring new space, you will need to tolerate frustration, difficulty and powerlessness without losing aim, without losing sight of what you're trying to accomplish, especially when faced with longer-term difficulties. Patience is the attitude that allows you to tolerate delay and suffering.

To achieve something you've never achieved before, you have to do things you've never done. And that usually means doing things that you're not good at, and that, in turn, usually means that you will fail from time to time. But that's okay, because every failed experiment is one step closer to success. It is one more piece of reality that we now have a perspective on, and it better informs us of what not to do and points us in the direction more accurately of what to do. (If you don't get set back, it's most likely because you're no trying something completely new, and/or you're not going into the unknown enough, because the territory you're in is not entirely unfamiliar.) So when you are trying to succeed, if you encounter problem after problem, obstacle after obstacle, stay strong; worthwhile things more often than not take time.

Patience and perseverance are two sides of the same coin, in the sense that perseverance is the proactive form of patience, which enables you to remain determined, without loss of effort or enthusiasm, despite having to endure difficulties and discouraging circumstances in pursuit of your goal. Patience and perseverance, in essence, is having the determination to navigate towards a goal despite any challenges, and to endure, no matter how much time it takes. Perseverance is what gets you up ten times when you have been knocked down nine. While exploring new space, you will need to tolerate frustration, difficulty, powerlessness and uncertainty without losing aim, without losing sight of what you're trying to accomplish, especially when faced with longer-term difficulties. The temperamental attitude of patience will help you preserve with your discovery of the know-how you are in search of, even when you are surrounded with uncertainty, pain, and suffering.

The capacity to accept and tolerate delay, problems, and suffering without becoming overwhelmed, annoyed or anxious to the point of giving up is absolutely crucial when trying to succeed. Your universal value of "why" will help you with patience and perseverance as it is your motivator.

> *"Patience is bitter, but the fruit is sweet."*
> *—Aristotle*

TEMPERAMENT #5: PLAYFULNESS

"The creation of something new is not accomplished by the intellect but by the play instinct."
—Carl Jung

The playful temperament involves openness to new perspectives, openness to surprise, and openness to the possibilities. You don't have to play to be playful, but you do have to be open and vulnerable, and you do have to let go of whatever rigid thoughts, feelings and ideas are holding you still and stopping your discovery.

Exploring, experimenting and fully engaging with objects around us is synonymous with play. It is common practice for children, and it is common practice amongst the most successful of adults. Those adults often use play as a way to interact what they do not yet know about, in order to discover more about the thing at hand.

Playfulness is all about yielding to the moment. Playfulness means presence and responsiveness, lightness and attentiveness, improvisation and creativity, a willingness to let go and become part of the new. There's nothing difficult about being playful. When you are playful, then you let go of all preconceived ideas that would otherwise stifle you. You are not even thinking about being in control or controlling anyone else; you're just thinking about fun. And if you see an opportunity, you take it, and if you see a possibility, you acknowledge it.

Play is often seen as childish and not having much purpose or value other than entertainment; however, play is not a pointless activity, and playfulness is certainly not a pointless temperament. Playfulness can serve as an extremely useful characteristic, especially when exploring new territory and new things; it not only promotes physical development of know-how, such as hand-eye coordination and physical skills, but it also develops cognitive know-how, such as solution finding, strategy formulations, etc., and social know-how, such as pair bonding, integrating into new groups, and so on.

Since play helps promote all of the above types of knowhow, it's easy to see how many problems it might help solve. For example, you might experiment or play with alternate ways of how you're going to earn money in order to find a solution to your money problems. Or you might play and imagine different ways in which you're going to surprise someone. This kind of playing and exploration of different solutions is synonymous with creativity (see more in "lateral thinking").

Being playful promotes flexibility of mind through adaptive engagement. You can play with your imagination to transcend what is known in your current state, by discovering new knowledge. Then you will discover many different ways to achieve the desired result.

"Almost all creativity involves purposeful play."
—Abraham Maslow

TEMPERAMENT #6: MINDFULNESS

"The best way to capture moments is to pay attention. This is how we cultivate mindfulness."
—Jon Kabat-Zinn

The temperament of mindfulness can best be conceptualized as having your complete attention on your present experience. Fully experiencing the input from your senses, feelings (emotions), and thoughts as they are collectively used will cultivate your understanding of your immediate environment.

Being mindful means orienting your awareness to your current experience, observing and attending to the everchanging field of experience (your thoughts, feelings and sensations). And you observe and attend to your experience from moment to moment by regulating and putting your attention on whatever you deem to be of most value. This temperament of mindfulness, this kind of attention to your immediate experience, allows for maximum recognition of events as they unfold in the present moment. And this is particularly useful when exploring new territory (a new space that you have not experienced before).

Being mindful is important because the present moment is where all opportunity lies and where all potential is born. If you are not mindful and paying attention to what's happening right now, in this very moment, you might miss the window of opportunity that is right in front of you, and it might be just the opportunity that you're in need of. This kind of awareness of the events as they unfold, and our emotional and thoughtful responses to what's unfolding now, allows for bigger space between the stimulus of the experience and a response to that stimulus, a space where we can make more well-informed decisions.

If you explore with this temperament of mindfulness, you will be more likely to adapt and learn at a rapid rate, because simply put, you are paying attention to the information in the present moment. And this information can then be utilized to develop self-awareness, self-knowledge and wisdom.

The keys to being mindful is to just notice each object that enters your stream of consciousness and to maintain an attitude of curiosity about the things you can sense, feel or think from moment to moment. (See tool #8: State, for more on how to become mindful).

> *"The little things? The little moments?*
> *They aren't little."*
> *—Jon Kabat-Zinn*

ADDITIONAL SUB-TEMPERAMENTS

"You can tell the size of a man by the size of the things that bother him."
—Adlai Stevenson

In addition to the essential temperaments that we've just reviewed, others can help with exploration.

Deliberation

When trying to find solutions to the challenges life has thrown at you, it's not always possible to go and explore straight away. And you don't have to, because you're capable of thinking. And exploration is what that thinking is: exploring the possibilities through thought, exploring new ideas and ways in order to discover what is useful and what is not.

And deliberation an ability to look far into the future. This kind of evaluation of cause and effect, foreseeing power struggles and successful pathways for action, is a great way to explore the possibilities and potential of the future. Especially when it's an extremely important matter that affects multiple people, we are more inclined to explore areas of the unknown more wisely based on utility and value. This kind of insight into the future unfolding of things, this characteristic of deliberation (thoughtful consideration) is built with experience and sophistication.

It's a trait that's effectiveness grows with time.

A deliberation is also what a quality conversation is: an exploration between people, where neither of you know yet where the conversation is going (because it's a new territory). And hopefully, by thinking out loud together and communicating well, you will become more well informed, helping each other discover more about the matter at hand.

Zest

Zest can be defined as approaching life as an adventure, living with a sense of excitement, energy, motivated by the challenges of the tasks ahead. Those who have zest exude enthusiasm, excitement and energy while approaching problems and difficulties in life.

The difference in effectiveness between those of us who are full of energy, who have that get up a go, who are full of zest, and those of us who aren't, can be huge, literally like night and day, worlds apart. It's not just a small amount of difference in terms of effectiveness; it is literally the difference of 100%!

Adding an intense, full of life and up-to-the-challenge kind of energy can be incredibly helpful when exploring and trying to overcome your challenges, because this type of energy, this type of enthusiasm can be the difference between winners and losers. If you live life with this sort of enthusiasm, you're much more likely to be active and proactive. Proactive people don't just sit back waiting for perfect circumstances or other people to help them overcome their challenges; instead, they go out and make the best out of their circumstances. This kind of energy is infectious as well, so that you will also be much more likely to gain help from others as a side benefit of your zest.

Living life zestfully involves performing tasks wholeheartedly, while also being adventurous, enthusiastic and energetic. Looking forward to each new day, you will want to fully participate in life, not just to view it from the sidelines. Knowing without doing is really just not knowing. So be proactive, and get out there and explore.

Sense of Humour

Having a sense of humour and laughing at yourself is good, because, in a sense, you're separating yourself from the part of you that made a mistake. And the part of you that is aware then transcends the mistake simply by being aware.

This disassociation with the part that made the mistake is empowering, and this empowering recognition fills you with a sudden increase of positive emotion. The part of you that is funny and often foolish and less than ideal is different from the part that recognized that what just happened was foolish or a mistake. And to the part of you that is foolish, which you find amusing, whatever happened, whatever caused the situation (perhaps you slipped, or something) is funny, because that part of you suddenly moved further away from the ideal. And the competitive part of you finds that funny, too, because now that you're aware of it, you're not likely to make that mistake again, and that's positive.

Positive emotions help people who are distressed to deal with what is occurring and to move forward and away from negative emotions. Also, positive emotions increase the probability of finding the good in future events. People who are high in emotional stability are those who are likely to experience more positive emotions as well, even in the face of stress. If you can cultivate these positive emotions, not just by laughing at yourself but at amusing events in general, it will not only help you cope with negative emotions but help you stay in a more positive, optimum state of being.

Having a sense of humour is what helps to cultivate positive, to stay hopeful and to cope with negative experiences, and even to create a better sense out of a situation by shifting your perspective. A sense of humour increases morale. It helps you tolerate repetitive tasks (too much activity in an explored area, for example) by introducing a little spontaneity into the routine. It even unleashes creativity by actively encouraging laughter and playful activities, which can further your solution-finding.

DISCOVER

"Every problem has a solution. You just have to be creative enough to find it."
—Travis Kalanick

Life is filled with unknowns, whether it be the incredibly familiar task of walking to the fridge to know what food is left inside or the incredibly overwhelming chaos of how you are going to manage living on past the death of loved ones. Exploring the unexplored terrain to discover the way we are needed to grow and to develop into more sophisticated versions of ourselves and to overcome life's hurdles.

A person who does not explore the unknown and the unexplored is or will become a naive, unaware and incompetent soul. The less experience and understanding, the weaker and more vulnerable the person will be. Exploration leads to understanding, and understanding leads to being capable (know-how).

TOOLS OF THE EXPLORER

"Even the simplest tools can empower people to do great things."
—*Biz Stone*

TOOLS

"I'm going to use all my tools, my God-given ability, and make the best life I can with it."
—Lebron James

Think about your tools. Do you know where your hammer, saws, and tapes are? (Or, if you are not into carpentry, what about your cooking utensils, your laptop, or paint palette?) Do you keep them well oiled, clean, organized and positioned, ready for you to use when you need them? Or do you just toss them aside, allowing them to gather dust and get rusty?

If you neglect your tools, they will decay and become worthless (useless). Either you won't find them, or they won't work when you need them most. However, if you look after them by keeping them well oiled, clean and organized, they will do their job correctly when you need them, saving you precious time and energy.

Remember: faulty tools produce poor results. And continual use of the same tools will produce the same poor results. A carpenter is only as good as the tools allow.

TOOL #1: QUESTIONS

*"Often, all that stands between you and what
you want is a better set of questions."*
—Tim Ferris

Questions help you explore. They shine a light (awareness) directly into the unknown. Questions immediately change what our awareness is focused on, and depending on what we are experiencing, they can change the way we think, feel and discover solutions. Asking empowering, resourceful and illuminating questions is one of the most powerful tools anyone can have when faced with a problem that has them not knowing what to do.

The unknown and not knowing is a part of life, and part of the way we deal with the not knowing is answering questions, It is crucially important to develop the habit of asking quality questions that are of value. A good question is one that, if answered, reveals something not known and of use.

Realizing the power of proper, precise, quality questions can give you the ability to change your state, change your social standing, change your current dilemma, etc. Good questions have the power to change the course of things into a more positive way.

There is a challenge with asking such high-quality questions, and which is that, if they are answered, they reveal the truth. And therein lies the problem, because some actually don't want to hear the truth. (Nothing hurts quite like the truth that you don't want to hear.) Therefore, you must be open to possibilities before asking the following problem-solving questions:

- What is bothering me?
- Why is this a problem?
- What is the best- and the worst-case scenario?
- Where would be most useful to explore?
- Where can I get more information on this topic?
- Where can I start improving things?
- Who could help me solve this problem?
- Is this situation something I could fix?
- What is this teaching me?
- What can I do to set things right, even just a bit?
- How am I going to resolve this?

- What's the most amount of good I can do in the shortest amount of time?
- What's the best thing I could do right now?
- What have I done that can be done in a better way?
- Am I doing anything that will make this worse?
- Am I speaking the truth the best know it?
- Am I doing useful things that are helping things progress?
- Is this my maximum effort?
- Am I giving in to comfort and laziness?
- Am I being responsible?
- Am I taking care of my responsibilities?
- Do I know why I'm doing this?
- Is the reason I'm doing this a good reason?
- Is fear stopping me?
- Do I have faith in what I'm doing is right and will produce the desired outcome?
- Do I expect this to work?
- Am I acting in a way that is aligned with what I believe?
- Is this good for now, and for tomorrow and next week and next month and for next year, etc....? If no, what is the duration of the solution I'm currently using?

- Will I feel good about this tomorrow?
- If solved, will it be good for me, and also good for my family and for others as well?

TOOL #2: LISTENING

"Most people don't listen with the intent to understand; they listen with the intent to reply."
—Stephen R. Covey

Listening to people helps us to problem-solve, because there is very little difference between thinking things through and talking things through. People don't often like thinking on its own, because it can be difficult, and so they don't think of solutions to solving their problems. If so, the best thing you can do is encourage those people to talk (so they think in the process), and the best way you can encourage that is by listening and paying attention to them. This is also extremely important when your own problems involve other people (as most problems do), because if you just listen, they might just tell you the problem.

There is very little difference between thinking and talking, and they are very highly correlated. Because they are both forms of turning the unknown into awareness by exploring them, whether this comes in the form of thinking or the form of thinking out loud with another, while paying close attention to their perspective as they explore.

This is a great part of the process of psychotherapy and counselling therapies. If someone talks, and they are exploring their problems as they tell you about it, then this exploration leads to new perspectives, cultivating new understandings, and unfolding into figuring things out, making sense of things and solution-finding. It's so important to listen to people, because you're giving them the gift of thinking things through and potentially finding solutions to their problems. And that's why it's so important for you to talk to the right person, to someone who is:

- listening,
- not judging,
- not interrupting, or
- not telling you what's what.

Then you can talk freely, which means thinking freely. Now you know the power of listening and can give this gift of listening to others. You can also choose who you talk to more wisely, knowing the value of talking to someone who listens.

Acknowledge that you don't know everything, so that the person you're talking with (if you listen to them and they listen to you) might have the know-how or information that you need. Most problems in life can be solved by listening combined with good company, and you'd be surprised how much you can learn and how much help you could acquire with that winning combination.

It's best to conceptualize your awareness as a bubble, with everything you're aware of and experience inside this bubble. Everyone else has a bubble too. It's helpful to view everything outside your bubble of awareness as information. All you've got to do is tune in to other people's awareness, and associate with people who will reciprocate, because some of that information might be the missing piece of your jigsaw puzzle.

Listen closely, with all your senses, to what is being shared with you. As well as doing good for them, you might pick something up that you didn't know that is good for you too. While you listen attentively, relevant associated thoughts will arise, and when it is your turn to speak, you can summarize these associations precisely, and communicate in a mutually beneficial way.

Your capacity for listening is reached when you can no longer summarize your thoughts as a response to what you're attentively listening to. To go beyond this point in listening will diminish the quality and value of your response. However, sometimes the most valuable thing that can be done in conversation is to continue listening, sacrificing your response and allowing the other simply to be completely heard.

The essence of listening is that you fully, deeply understand the other person, emotionally as well as intellectually. In order to sustain this level of listening:

- Give your physical, psychological and emotional attention to another person.
- Display that you are listening with steady eye contact, verbal expressions of encouragement, a relaxed posture of involvement, and with appropriate body motion (nodding, for example).

- Don't be quick to judge.
- Don't just wait for your turn to speak, but pay attention.
- Recognize and accept that some things take time to communicate and explain.

TOOL #3: WRITING

"If people cannot write well, they cannot think well, and if they cannot think well, others will do their thinking for them."
—George Orwell

As we know, because we are creatures with thinking ability (the ability to abstract), we don't need to always physically travel anywhere to explore, and we can explore with our thoughts and imagination. That's what abstraction means, passively exploring in mind, in the context of your thoughts. Thinking is a problem-solving simulation). Simulation is where you can run scenarios, explore, evaluate the causeand- effect chain that you uncover before you actually do something in the real world.

When we think (explore) freely, we are likely to have whispers of insights, thoughts and inclinations that are incredibly useful. But they are quick like whispers in the wind. One minute they're there and the next they're gone. A whisper of insight can be very hard to catch and remember in the forefront of our minds, especially when we have things going on in our day-to-day lives that might distract us. And then the "Eureka!" moments of insight are lost.

If you want to be able to capture these moments of inspiration, you can do it by writing them down on paper. That piece of paper can hold more thoughts than you can hold in the forefront of your conscious mind. How many thoughts can you hold in mind at one moment in time? Perhaps two, maybe three at a stretch. You can, however, write them down clearly and precisely put them on the paper, and then start the process again of abstract in exploring thoughts. And when you have another idea, you can capture that one on paper as well. Eventually you will be left with a paper filled with brilliant ideas, goals, problem-solving formulas, etc.

Then, when you've completed your mental simulations, you can stop thinking, and you can interact with them in reality and start putting your ideas into actual practical use. You can see them from a new perspective when they're on the paper. This method of writing things down and holding your thoughts on paper allows you to more easily make sense of things.

Writing is also helpful because it is very similar to thinking and talking as it is a form of exploration (see the "Listening" tool). There is also not much difference between thinking and talking and writing; they follow the mental process that governs formalization and clarification, the process of making things understood and clearly identified, so that we can then compartmentalize them in memory. The process of talking about things the process of thinking. The process of writing also helps you make sense and understand things. If you just take the time to do so, the perspectives and insights that are possible to gain from writing are immeasurable.

Here's how to write:

- Write, freely describing exactly what thoughts pop into your mind. The goal here is to produce, not to assess, just to produce and to flow. Right unfiltered about whatever pops into your mind about the subject at hand.
- Next, break down into sections and sentences everything that you have written down. Separate each sentence into distinct parts, so it's easy to clarify each part of your thought.

- Now it's time to edit to make your ideas clear. Formalize and review each sentence and each thread that you've written down, trying to make clearer, more precise and more particular what it is you're trying to understand.

- Re-edit, repeating Steps 2 and 3. Read your writing again, and repeat Steps 2, 3 and 4 until your idea is as clear and as concise and articulate as possible.

- If you've done this process, you should not only have tracked your ideas and put them into existence, but you should have a better understanding and perspective on matters at hand. The usefulness of this type of capturing and evaluating and making sense of things is infinitely useful and will help you to make sense of a problem.

- Use models and diagrams as well, to help yourself break down, explore and navigate your thoughts on paper.

TOOL #4: LATERAL THINKING

"If you never change your mind, why have one?"
—Edward De Bono

Lateral thinking is a way of generating alternative solutions and the more solutions you have, the more likely you are to find and use the best most effective solution. To think laterally, you must suspend your judgement, because it will impede your ability to explore ideas and other opinions because the new idea may not at first seem useful. At this stage, you are not putting anything into practice, and perhaps not even engaging in a mental simulation. You are only creating possible solutions.

Lateral thinking is exploration without reference to where you are going (the specific outcome in mind). The goal is simply to experience and discover different ways of operating and interacting within the space (territory) where your problem resides. This approach to problem-solving means approaching problems indirectly at diverse angles of perspective, instead of concentrating on the subtle details of one particular approach for a length of time.

Instead of focusing on the details of your current approach, lateral thinking is about finding answers to problems by considering the possibility of attack using different tools and/or using those tools in different ways than originally intended. This way of approaching problems is how you get "outside the box". This type of reasoning is not immediately obvious, and your emotions might not support you, because you might not feel the same sense of progress as in a stepby- step logical approach. However, *the "light bulb moments" and quantum leaps in progress almost always come from this type of "outside the box" approach to problem-solving.*

To think laterally,

- Search for different perspectives on the matter at hand, and then embody the different interpretation and tools of that perspective.
- Search for different methods of preparation, technology, tools and other ways that might be used to solve different

problems, which you might be able to transfer and utilize to approach your challenges.

- Use randomness and chance to enhance your exploration of new unexplored ways and perspectives. If you learn about a new approach or idea, take a moment to focus and reflect.

"From where we stand, the rain seems random. If we could stand somewhere else, we would see the order in it."
—Tony Hillerman

TOOL #5: MENTORS

*"Role models who push us to exceed our limits,
physical training that removes our spare tires, and risks
that expand our sphere of comfortable action are all
examples of eustress: stress that is healthful
and the stimulus for growth."*
—Tim Ferris

A mentor teaches and demonstrates. Because you won't always have much time to explore and learn on your own, so your own learning can be limited to the time available. However, you can save time, resources and energy with proper guidance. This is why it's incredibly useful to have mentors to provide guidance, advice, emotional support, encouragement. Without mentors, you could unnecessarily waste time, resources and money.

Having a mentor-mentee, a student-teacher, or a master-apprentice type of relationship with those who are more competent and experienced can be one of the most productive forms of learning, helping you to discover know-how and to solve your problems. The sophistication and know-how of the mentor will become yours, if you are a good student and the mentor is wise. A mentor offers precise and accurate feedback on your efforts, ideally in real-time, allowing you to more rapidly improve and become sophisticated.

Finding the appropriate mentor is important, It's best, if possible, to deliberately choose your mentors, and you should choose someone who best suits your needs. We are finite creatures and do not know it all, so it is incredibly useful to have a mentor who can offer knowledge. Build a relationship with someone who is more competent and experienced, and who is willing to teach you what they "know-how" to do. We might even have a mentor in every area of our lives.

Mentoring and teaching others yourself, when the opportunity arises, is also a great way to "sharpen your own saw" and to keep on top of your own understanding. Taking the time to help others by explaining and instructing is an effective way to gain new perspectives through their struggles and difficulties, by helping them the know-how to overcome and solve their problems.

You don't have to be a full-time mentor to reap the benefits from teaching others, and you don't have to have a full-time mentee to reap the usefulness of having someone more knowledgeable nearby. Helping opportunities to share or to acquire knowledge present themselves all the time, such as not quite knowing how to do a particular something at work, and then asking someone who does to quickly show you how. Or teaching your kids how to solve a problem in their math homework. Or helping someone else who is struggling with something you've already resolved.

TOOL #6: MONEY

"Money is a very important tool to make a big difference in people's lives. It is positive or negative depending on the values."
—Shiv Khera

Money is a problem, or the lack of it is a problem for most of us, at least at some point or another in our lives. But if used correctly, and even in small amounts, it can prove to be an incredible tool for manifesting desired results.

Money is a tool, like a hammer. You can use a hammer to build a house or destroy a house. Regardless of how you use it, the hammer itself is merely a tool. The person using the hammer is responsible for its effects.

Money contains potential; it is potential exchanged between people. More specifically, it is positive potential that is yet unspent, Which can unlock know-how more easily than you might without that potential.

Ultimately, to be used most effectively, money should be used in ways that are in line and accordance to the "Universal Values" (you might want to take a moment now to review that section). If you don't use money in a way that is bad for you, then you're not likely to waste it on expedient, yet useless or meaningless, things, which become a waste at a later date. Instead, through values, you can spend money on things that reveal deeper truths, and are useful in the long term, such as books, education, tools, and the obvious stuff, like food and shelter, then that's likely to be good for you and others.

Money can be used to manifest any other practical tool in existence, and even those that don't currently exist. So,

if you're disciplined,

if you won't waste it,

if you are responsible with it,

if you use it wisely, and if you do the maximum good with it that you can, then you are highly likely to become a very wealthy individual who creates positive change in the world by solving vast amounts of money-related problems.

"An investment in knowledge pays the best interest."
—*Benjamin Franklin*

TOOL #7: SACRIFICE

"Great achievement is usually born of great sacrifice,
and is never the result of selfishness."
—Napoleon Hill

A sacrifice is arguably the most powerful tool there is. Sacrifice means giving up something that you already have, or that you want, for something else that is even better.

If you stop moving forward in life. It's usually because you are attached to things that you should no longer be attached to if you are to solve your current problems. And if you are not moving forward, it's likely because you have some idea, mode of action, or other habit that you won't let go of that's holding you back.

That said, the trick to sacrifice is to find that part of yourself that is holding you back and let it go. Perhaps, for example, it's your self-image, because you are worried about what people will think. Maybe it's that you've got the wrong ideals in mind.

Perhaps it's your comfort zone, and perhaps it's even a love for expedient pleasure.

The bigger the goal, usually, the harder and more challenging it is to solve the problems and obstacles. Which, in turn, usually means the bigger the sacrifice is required from you. So if you are hungry, then you might only have to sacrifice the comfort of your bed to get up and get food from the fridge. However, if you want to build a rocket to fly to Mars and back, the problems would seem nearly endless. You are going to have to sacrifice a lot of time, money and effort and ego and comfort and just about everything near and dear to you in order to achieve space flight.

Your chosen sacrifices should be in accordance with the universal values, always. It's important to note that you should not sacrifice things that will cause a decrease in the well-being of yourself or others, unless perhaps that sacrifice takes the form of delayed gratification, because you truly believe that the future will be better and have more well-being for yourself and all that are involved.

Again, sacrifice is a three-step process: 1) figure out what is holding you back from progress, 2) let it go, and 3) proceed and progress.

> *"If you don't sacrifice for what you want,*
> *what you want becomes the sacrifice."*
> —*Joubert Botha*

TOOL #8: STATE

"The number one key to success in life is to master your own state. If you can manage and master your states, there's nothing you can't do."
— Tony Robbins

Your state is the physical, mental and emotional aspects of being, and, at times, we can all end up in a negative way of being, a negative state. However, there are ways of changing your state of being. Being able to change your state of being is one of the best indirect ways of increasing your problem-solving ability. Because if you are in a peak physical, emotional and mental state, then you are more likely to perform well as a person, particularly in your problem-solving.

Here are things you can explore, or perhaps do better ,that will most definitely improve your state of being.

Diet

What you eat has a direct, major effect of how you feel and

therefore, likely to influence how you behave and perform. A boxer doesn't prepare for the tremendous problem-solving task of the fight by eating un-nourishing food, and neither should you. Eat a well-balanced diet, nutrient and proteinrich. Make sure your body is nourished with all the nutrients it needs to function properly. If your body isn't fed right, it will not be able to make all the hormones that are needed for you to feel good and think straight. So if you are depleted, you will make it harder and more difficult for yourself to get into a good state. Hydration is also incredibly important to your physical and mental well-being and performance.

Exercise

Your body's condition has a major effect on how capable you are of maintaining a positive high-energy state, and, therefore, is likely to influence how you behave and perform. If you are physically not capable of sustaining high energy for any useful amounts of time, then your willpower is most likely going to be spent trying to motivate yourself, challenges. So please stay in relatively good condition (physical health).

Sleep

Being well-rested has a significant effect on your state. If you are sleep-deprived, your body will likely not have recovered and repaired itself physically, emotionally and mentally from the day before. Most adults need between 6 and 9 hours of sleep every night. If you've under slept, you will still be exhausted and fatigued from the day before. To prevent this, first, keep well-ordered sleeping hours. This programs the brain and internal body clock, to get used to a set routine. By working out what time you need to wake up, and then set a regular sleep schedule.

It also might seem like a good idea to try to catch up on sleep after a late night. However, doing so on a regular basis can also disrupt your sleep routine. Travel can also interrupt this rhythm.

Posture Check

There are a lot of good reasons to aim for good posture. There is a relationship between posture and how you feel emotionally. Good posture can even influence your emotional state and your sensitivity to pain.

If you stand in power poses just (think "superheroes"), you will begin to feel more confident and in command. If you gesture and hold yourself in an open and loving way your emotions will begin to follow suit soon after. Check your posture and expressions the next time you're feeling negative. Then embody more positive posture and expressions, and your emotional and mental state will rise.

Meditation

Meditation is a practice which you can use to achieve a mentally clear and emotionally calm and stable state. This is particularly useful when in a state of anxiety or any other high-energy, yet negative state.

Every experience you've ever had and every emotion, whether you felt it yesterday, or ten years ago, doesn't have to remain. Meditation helps you cultivate the ability to return to a neutral, stable state with mental clarity. It doesn't necessarily prevent negative emotions and thoughts, because they are a part of life, but it does let them slip away more quickly and prevent them from consuming you. This ability to escape the grip of ruminating thoughts about the already known problems, and anticipation of the unknown can make all the difference in your state, and thus with your problem-solving. A great way to meditate is to focus on controlling your breathing, inhaling and exhaling slowly and deeply. This pattern helps draw your attention and awareness from your overwhelming thoughts and feelings, centering and resetting yourself to a calm yet wakeful state.

Embodiment

Your emotional state and your actions have an influencing effect on each other. For example, if you feel strong, you are very likely to behave in a strong manner. And if you act in a calm and composed manner, even when you feel scared and agitated, you will begin to feel calm and composed. Embodying the state you desire useful when you find yourself in the middle of an uncertain situation that's causing anxiety and uncertainty, because we all can often feel overwhelmed or tired or whatever subpar state.

We can use this knowledge to change our state of being and fill ourselves with more positive emotions and actions. If you feel like you're stuck in second gear, unable to muster any enthusiasm, and there is some challenge ahead of you that you need to perform, use this tool: stand up, breathing in deeply and commanding yourself to energize, and then begin moving as you need to move, just going through the motions despite how you are thinking and feeling. Eventually your emotions will follow your actions.

Gratitude

Gratitude can be just what is needed to lift your state when you find yourself in a negative attitude. Gratitude affirms the good things we've received, acknowledging and making us aware of the good things in our lives, especially the role other people play in providing our lives with goodness. And that awareness has a tremendous impact on your state of being. Gratitude works best when you practice being kind. You can do that by giving thanks and expressing your appreciation for the good things in your life and by expressing thanks or reciprocating the good done for you.

WEAPONS

*"Education is the most powerful weapon which
you can use to change the world."*
—Nelson Mandela

These tools are your weapons against not knowing. They will help you discover what to do when you don't know what to do. They will help you in general, but are particularly useful when facing what you want but don't know 'how-to' achieve. Use them well!

MODUS VIVENDI

"If you don't try, you won't know."
—Attributed to many sages

What is an explorer?

- An adventurer

- A hero

- An actualizer

- A proactive creator

- A problem solver

- A fully functioning person

- A pioneer

- An experimenter

- A traveller

- A discoverer

Someone who can create something out of nothing.

Explorers voluntarily approach and engage a problem. They do not hide from uncertain situations. They confront, they contend, and they learn from their challenging encounters; and then they reengage, new, improved and more wellinformed than before. They accept the truth and information that gets discovered in the new situation, they re-orient and calibrate themselves, and then they explore again, in a more sophisticated and effective way.

Explorers can transform. They might not be capable of success today, but they will transform into someone who is capable tomorrow. They are learning machines, capable of transforming themselves and the environment.

This book has given you the tools, skills and values that can change your life. You have come a long way and learned a lot. How much further you go is up to you. When you put this book down, you can make efforts to take control of your own life by solving and overcoming your problems and challenges. You now know the universal values that will help you navigate unexplored territory, properly. You now know the importance of exploring new things, and you can create goals when it comes to discovering the solutions you need. You now know what temperaments and attitudes to embody when doing new things. Finally, you now know what practices will improve your ability to discover know-how and to accelerate your learning curves.

Remember: every time you are faced with a problem, you are simultaneously faced with an adventure and a learning opportunity.

There is so much adventure in front of you, so much opportunity, so much to explore and discover, and so much to enjoy. Look forward to the adventure, because you are up to the challenge!

ABOUT THE AUTHOR

Albie Wake lives the life of an explorer. Continually learning new things and striving to improve himself and the world around him. Albie shares what he has learned so others can unlock their potential and improve their lives and the world around them too.

He currently lives in south London

You can contact author Albie Wake at:

Email: albiewake@gmail.com

Instagram @albiewake

Post pictures of your favourite pages, quotes and experiences related to this book on Instagram using #albiewake so he can like them and feature them on his Instagram.